I S

EQUALITY

A N

ABSOLUTE

GOOD

?

First Paul Dry Books Edition, 2022

Paul Dry Books, Inc.
Philadelphia, Pennsylvania
www.pauldrybooks.com

Printed in the United States of America

ISBN 978-1-58988-163-1

IS

EQUALITY

AN

ABSOLUTE

GOOD

?

EVA BRANN

PAUL DRY BOOKS

Philadelphia 2022

...with this epoch also began the inequality among human beings, this rich source of so much evil but also all good.

—IMMANUEL KANT, "Conjectural Beginning of Human History" (1785)

After all, the scales can show "equal" when the weighing pans of the balance are empty.

Regarding the title: 1. The question mark expresses a genuine perplexity on my part. I am at once a true believer and real apostate. 2. By "Absolute Good" I mean good-in-itself.

In childhood I was passionate about getting my exact half (though I did not refuse a larger share) of whatever good thing was on offer. My mother, a Solomonic judge, had a solution. I, the elder, cut the wedge of cake; my little brother chose. No two halves were ever more equal.

Even in old age I think that dispensations and distributions are better off with the most achievable equality. The most serious secular example would be the equality of justice under law. But even in very insignificant situations, the desire for equal treatment is almost a reflex.

If I am having lunch with a colleague and his hamburger comes with a sour pickle, then so must mine, whether I want it or not. This trivial requirement is thus to be interpreted as a desire for equality rather than for pickles.

It might be said that not egalitarianism but fairness is at stake in this niggling example. Fairness, however, is an acknowledgement of just deserts, and therefore implies equality in dealings with similarly entitled partners. So it is indeed equality adjusted to circumstances that I desire. Thus there is an intimation that equality will come into play when justice is administered communally. When, however, it is to be meted out individually, as in one-child families or in our relation to the deity, the emphasis may be more on the appropriateness of the dispensation, to fitness rather than equity.

In our ordinary, not very reflective, lives, we middle-class Americans live in sanguine expectation of equal treatment—those of us, at least, who are not activists by temperament. That is because most of our approved public rhetoric, if not always our actual conduct, is in favor of the equal worth of individuals—equal because human being is *in*valuable, thus priceless in both senses: inestimable quantitatively and beyond all price qualitatively.

Yet in totalitarian countries equality is, if anything, even more scrupulously observed, not, however, in a Whitmanesque spirit of camaraderie. It is, instead, because in countries where there is dearth of dignity and plenty of poverty, people derive a desperate satisfaction from at least seeing all but their leaders in their identical situation. And they tolerate their officials flaunting their wealth, while in free countries the rich often mask their wealth by casual dress and amiable behavior.

Thus happy equals, who understand the essentially immeasurable and uncountable nature of human being, view equality as a fall-back term. What they really mean is "quantitatively incomparable"—while the wretched equals of the unfree world take some small comfort from belonging to a mass of equally miserable comrades.

Equality is a social relation of mutuality. Actually, "mutually equal" is redundant since mutuality is part of the concept of equality. Equality, be it of people or of things, *means* being equal *to* one another. But more: to be equal to another necessitates that this other be equal to its other *simultaneously*. To me, mutuality implies contemporaneity. Hence it is inaccurate to think of equality as reciprocal, as a responsive turn-and-turn-about relation. This distinction is not "merely semantic," but, like many small signifying distinctions, it can have considerable real-life effects.

In the case of equality there is indeed such an effect. For if the relation of equality is conceived as involving reciprocity, then, in the sphere of "social" justice, wherever an inequality is observed, there rectification, equalization, will be demanded. Now if—this phenomenon will turn up again, see below under "envy"—the privileged partner complies, the receiving partner will complain of being "patronized." Thus for people intent on "doing the right thing" a "damned if you do, damned if you don't" situation is apt to arise.

Now in well-working democratic republics like America—people who cavil with this judgment tend to have no experience of really ill-conditioned countries— one epiphenomenon, or no, rather an enabling factor, of this spontaneous rather than *dirigiste* equality is a general civility, a civic courtesy, ranging from the folksy joviality alluded to above to the punctilious according of honorifics; it is, for example, almost impossible to persuade the public not to promote any academic they meet to "Professor." [1]

These American ceremonies of informality are mostly semi-conscious and habitual. Yet on occasion they show themselves to be more than manners, to be the surface of a deeper, active humanity. I've heard it said that the pervasively courteous kindness of our casual social life is the froth on our not particularly meritorious safety and prosperity; it will not withstand hard times. Well, it's doing it right now (2021, Year 2 of Covid-19). But it may, indeed, well be that helpful conduct owes more to a democratic social mode, to its natural goodheartedness and natural good manners, than to moral conviction—that this very fact renders it more resilient. Those of us who sometimes wonder what makes people good will recognize this concern as a version of the grand question: What is the practical effect of belief (consciously thought-out opinion) or faith (the conviction that there is a supervising divinity) on practical action?

By and large, I'm a happy participant in egalitarian democratic life, even a true believer, since, for all its low propensities, I know of no actualizable better way. So these congenial ways are not the cause of my perplexed apostasy. That stems from a lot of public rhetoric in favor of *mere* equality, equality not as a way to enough but as a good in itself, even as a path to political redemption.

For somewhere in these claims there lurks a flight from substance to relation. I mean the fellow citizens who pontificate in public often don't feel called upon or even entitled to flesh out their egalitarian devotion with specifications in compellingly concrete detail of

IS EQUALITY AN ABSOLUTE GOOD?

the good life that will ensue once equality is achieved. I've seen this in our students: a sort of pernicious modesty that protects them from opposition, but even before that, relieves them from a strenuous bout of thoughtful imagining.[2] Then the fall-back position is to retreat from positive envisioning to relational calculation. It's our teacherly job to call them on this flabbiness.

This retreat from substance turns me, by temperament a friendly populist, to apostasy. I am repelled by the politics that I term to myself "principled egalitarianism," since I think that equality should *not* be an approved political principle.

So let me say up front what points I'll try to make plausible, since an essay of opinion, unlike a murder mystery, does not gain by leaving the reader suspended up to the final revelation. I shall argue that our political rhetoric would be sounder if calls for more equality, unqualified by the good of it, were replaced by commitments to *enough*, to *sufficient* for all. And particularly so if these calls had been accompanied by outrage at any appearance of inequality.[3] It seems to me a sober, achievable goal that all should have *enough* to sustain life, *sufficient* to enable liberty, and *adequate* to enter the pursuit of happiness. Mute equality, and, I think this follows, speak the clearer for fellow feeling.

So again: Our political speech would be more candid and more practical if we replaced calls for equalization with attention to sufficiency and, substituting "enough" for "equal," let inequality reign—within wide limits.

I've just appealed to our Declaration of Independence for specifying the respects in which we should be taxed to supply citizens (and residents) with enough, if they can't get it on their own. And suppose that this does make for higher taxes, so be it.

Suppose that other Americans have more than I do, exponentially to the umptieth power more, what is that to me? unless they engage in nefarious activities, in which case, we being equal under the law, Lock 'em up! But I hasten to qualify the above. Inordinate, gross inequality is probably a political, certainly a social, evil. But we are better entitled to affirm that if we have thought out just why such inequality is wrong.

One reason is that very grossness, which sits ill on the American body politic whose very constitution is a naturally well-bred sobriety. Another is that, as I observed above, having read it in Tocqueville, the American rich, far from flaunting *themselves*, tend to go incognito—or used to.[4] Its beneficiaries seem to understand that such excess is, as we tend to say, so as not to seem judgmental, "inappropriate" to our democratic mores, although that sort of natural tact and unforced courtesy has, under the media-enabled celebrity culture, fallen largely into abeyance. Thus our students have, without losing their goodheartedness, declined somewhat in manners. One more argument against inequality—perhaps ultimately more against the excess itself—is that it endangers the possessors themselves, morally and sometimes physically (see Note 4). And finally, though there are many other evils to great excess, the one most dangerous to the polity itself, the arrogation of political power by the unelected—even if, or even especially if, it works well. For example, huge, well-run media companies can exercise censorship (albeit right-minded) forbidden to the elected Congress by the First Amendment to our Constitution.[5]

The ultimate argument against really inordinate inequality is its depressive effect on human activity, and so on happiness. I am going here by Aristotle's understanding of happiness, which accords with my experience: Happiness overtakes us when the soul is fully at work in an excellent way—for instance, putting its all into getting a feel for and an understanding of equality, what it is and isn't.[6] If we are continually leaned on by the inordinacy of huge inequality, one of two consequences seem to me possible. We may give in to our insignificance and cede our souls' activity to resignation and give up work, or we may become psychic guerillas by going into a heroic mode and become aggressive. Heroism, however, is not conducive to working things out; it is too strenuous, actually too contractedly defensive for the relaxed tension which is the mood for inquiry, when the inner watchman sings out "Twelve o'clock (it often is) and all's well." It is the time when the multitude of duty-imposed distractions goes unheeded.

All in all, an overt conservativism of the sort that used to be called (looking to the positive rather than the merely preserving side of conservatism) liberalism, classical liberalism, speaks to and for me as I try my hand in praise of a bounded inequality.[7]

> *And when we got too far apart in wealth,*
> *'Twas his idea that for the public health,*
>
> *So that the poor won't have to steal by stealth,*
> *We now and then should take an equalizer.*

It's from some rhymes—you can't call it poetry— by Robert Frost, called "The Equalizer." We're not told who "he" is; he seems to be both a person who gives us an idea and a pill we take. The lines contain the social argument against inordinate inequality, crime; the personal evils don't need cataloguing, from the arrogance of the better endowed to the demeaning of the poorer.

When we try to think out the meaning of a term it is good to have a serious grounding text at hand. There is such a one, the grandest of all, our Declaration of Independence. It is, of course, first an announcement of a rightful rebellion, called a revolution, but it is also both an idea-fraught exposition of equality and the occasion of its institution as a founding principle for a new nation—for the Declaration is also Public Law No. 1.

In taking the Declaration of 1776 as more than a political act for the day, as a text to be interpreted for the ages, a thought-laden and -provoking writing on equality and its delimitations, I am committing myself to some hermeneutic, that is, interpretational analysis of the pertinent part, the sentence that immediately follows the opening prelude and the peroration with which the document concludes.

In fact, let me speak to that proud concluding promise out of order. First, because, in its pregnant beauty, it is so particularly amenable to my approach, which is to read the words literally and to ask what they mean and what I think they are meant to mean.

The Founding Fathers "mutually pledge to each other"—a redundancy meant, I think, for a reiteration—over their signatures, "our Lives, our Fortunes, and our sacred Honor." Note that these pledges echo, though more distantly as they go, the rights announced at the beginning: Life, Liberty, Pursuit of Happiness. Lives and fortunes are each in some connection with Life and Liberty— for fortunes bestow freedoms, material independence. But the Pursuit of Happiness and sacred Honor are, it might even be said, worlds apart, for the one promises indulgence and the other sacrifice. We might even ask: Is "sacred Honor" actually compatible with citizenship in a democracy, the first article of whose Constitution proscribes titles of nobility? Are the Founders of a different breed from the citizens they are constituting?

It seems to me, then, that courage and liberality, the consecration of their physical being and their material wealth, contain no inconsistency. The pledge, however, of their sacred honor offers difficulties: What reverence (sacredness) and nobility (honor) would be in tune with the democratic mode? Can meritorious distinction not of this or that particular act but of one's very being be acceptable to egalitarian convictions?

Was the theoretical adherence of the Founders perhaps sometimes at odds with their personal sense of themselves? I feel emboldened to ask because Abraham Lincoln, who is at once the most genuine and safest of populists and the grandest of public figures, asked, in his youth, that very question: Can the ambition of "Towering genius that disdains the beaten path" subject itself to democratic mediocrity?[8] I'll leave that question, which calls up aspects of an incipient tragedy, unanswered, except for one comment: Lincoln did find for himself a path neither worn out nor errant. For all that, I'll put my essay under the aegis of Lincoln's question.

Certainly the end of the Declaration raises Lincoln's very quandary—and, of course, it was a personal perplexity he was making public, a warning against himself!

But back to the beginning. My college occasionally invites local high schoolers and their teachers to join us in a seminar, by which we mean, simply, a text-based conversation.[9] I volunteered to lead such a one and was invited to propose a text. I chose the Declaration. Clearly dominant in this class of seniors, both in all three physical dimensions and in intellectual initiative, was a young black man, who, in response to my opening question, asked modestly but self-confidently if he might replace it with his own. "Be my guest," I said and he asked: "It says here that all men are *created* equal, and that they are endowed by their *creator* with all these rights. What if they don't believe in God and don't think they're his creatures?"[10] "But what?" I asked, already enchanted— what more crucial question could there be than that about faith in the purported guarantor of equality Himself? He gave the expected answer: "Oh, evolution and all that." He was evidently trusted by his classmates because they began to try to answer, some boldly, some shyly.

This problem soon came forward: The author, Jefferson, thinks that "We hold these truths to be self-evident." Which truths? Jefferson says:

> *We hold these truths to be self-evident that all*
> *men are created equal, that they are endowed by*
> *their Creator with certain unalienable Rights,*
> *that among these are Life, Liberty, and the pur-*
> *suit of Happiness.*

Does he mean that God created human beings first and in themselves equal, and then, having given them a creation that made them each other's equal, he, additionally, gave them an indefinite number of unenumerated rights, saving out three, presumably the most fundamental ones, to specify? *Or* does Jefferson mean that God created men not as first of all *being equal* to each other but as being *equally endowed* with rights, being in possession of an equal number of the same rights?

The difference is not "merely semantic." It is a difference in the conception underlying our democracy. Are we first and above all, in our very being, related to each other on equal terms, and then gifted with superadded rights, or does our equality begin and end with our being similarly possessed of the same rights? For example, is our differentiation as individuals nugatory in the face of our first-created equality, or are we in our very creation distinguished from each other by "distinctions," both in the sense of mere differences and of degrees of merit? (From here on I am reporting more my own lucubrations than our guests'.)

"Self-evident" needs to be considered. What does it mean? *Self* is a reflexive term: "It, itself." *Evident* means "highly visible." *E* and *ex-* raise the term to which they are prefixed, as in "extol." It must be something like "seeing is believing," or "to hear is to be convinced." Usually an argument, a proof, mediates between a proposed enunciation and the term to be truth-certified. So what term in the Declaration's first sentence is such that just to see what it denotes is to know it indeed to be the case? What is "very visibly so," just by being its own self, unaided by supporting evidence or rational validation—which indeed is lacking in the Declaration. Instead Jefferson refers to a causal agent, the creating deity, whom to mention is supposed to obviate all proof.

So arises a second question: What is it that is self-evident? It seemed undecidable whether Jefferson meant that we are primarily fundamentally and independently equal—*homo aequus* as much as *homo sapiens*, or perhaps more so—and then, secondarily endowed with certain rights. But it is clear, I think, that self-evidence extends over the whole first sentence: The text refers to a plurality of truths as self-evident, and the Creator is operative both in according the property of equality and the endowment of rights (be it sequentially or simultaneously). So surely all the propositions into which one may decompose the sentence are under the aegis of "self-evident."

Third question: To whom is all this self-evident? To us. Jefferson writes, "*We* hold…" He regarded the document as "an expression of the American Mind." Thus we Americans in general will agree with its principles. Nonetheless, only some, the radical egalitarians, will agree with one reading, that equality is inherent in us. On the other hand, we all, as Americans, really ought to believe that we are endowed with certain irremovable rights, and we might say that it's by nature. Though I myself *can't quite believe* that I was naturally *born* to Jeffersonian rights; yet I do believe it's a better country if we all behave as if each of us was thus well-endowed by nature, merely by being born.

But I do *know for sure*, as against the absolute egal-itarians, that we are not in their sense equal, not defin-able as near-identical with all other human beings and so always on the brink of collapsing into indiscernible identity—from which only my identification with some prescribed tribe, be it gender, sexual preference, race, religion, ethnicity, can rescue me.

So I think that even a very moderately thoughtful person, even fairly young children, show in their be-havior that surviving, moving freely, securing goods are simply in their make-up, and that Jefferson did well to enumerate these three that they have along with every-one else. Incidentally, "pursuit" in this context did not mean a "chase" but a practice; Jefferson probably really meant that we have a right, so to speak, to ply happiness like a vocation.[11] Moreover, he evidently thought that we each know what makes us happy and that "Governments are instituted to secure" our happiness. Yet the common present reading, that we should have the opportunity to go after happiness, seems to fit our condition better; the transition of the term's meaning from "job" to "quest" curiously tracks the way of enterprise.

It has its darker side: Happiness is pursued because it is fugitive. For the underprivileged that is because opportunity is not equal, but for the secure middle class it is often because we live in confusion concerning the essence of happiness. I know of two extremes in the delineation of happiness: Aristotle, cited above, who says that happiness is the soul well at work, and Hobbes who says:

> *Felicity is a continual progress of desire, from one object to another; the attaining of the former, being still but the way to the latter.*[12]

The unhappiness of the too many fairly well-off Americans is, I am guessing, often ascribable to their having absorbed the Hobbesian dictum (which exactly fits the pursuit/chase meaning), though probably not from that source.

How does this Jeffersonian interlude bear on the anti-egalitarian argument I am pursuing? Well, if Jefferson, the most egalitarian of the Founders, can't quite sustain his monogamous attachment to equality, then perhaps it's not so easily sustainable. In fact, wherever I look I see variation, not only difference in kind but inequality of merit.

Where then do we look for evidence of our human constitution's parity (or disparity)? Does our equality perhaps come to us from our common biological classification, are we taxonomically equalized? Well, Socrates denies it. Being *homo sapiens* does not make us equally sapient. Our animal-being, even our body's innards look pretty much alike, and yet our souls may differ *toto caelo,* by a whole heaven.[13] So neither through creation by a Father in heaven, nor by adherence to the Founding Fathers' truths, nor by evolution from Forefathers on earth are we made truly in the image of Frost's equalizers. They belong to the American scene from way back and do just the opposite of the self-perverting demon of Goethe's *Faust*, who always wants evil and always achieves good: They goodheartedly wreak havoc.

Back one last time to Jefferson. When he speaks of our endowment with certain rights, are there any among them that belong to some or fail to belong to them by reason of their superiority or inferiority? I think we all know what Jefferson meant—though maybe not, as Frost says in "The Black Cottage": That's a hard mystery of Jefferson's—that we are all equally endowed with the rights mentioned or alluded to and are so endowed by reason of our equal human creation. As I've pointed out, Jefferson was not reliable as an egalitarian (Note 13), nor was he reliable as a believer in God. But it doesn't much matter. For he is speaking of political rights, where the claim carries conviction on merely prudential grounds, quite aside from the possibly partly pretended, yet in a great cause rhetorically justifiable, expression of belief.

But mustn't there be, in the personal realm, rights that accrue precisely by reason of personal uniqueness, of being superior, "past compare"—accrue precisely

because of his being incomparably himself to someone? So in political relations rights may be grounded
in equality, which operates through comparison, but in
amorous relations the most acute attraction lies in being
beyond comparison, incomparably individual.

Let me here take a moment to say a few words about
the way I've approached the Declaration, a document.
Usually what Jefferson (aided, among others, by Adams
and Franklin) meant is clear—because, not in spite of, the
ambiguities. Exactitude would have required prolixity
and induced suspicion. He was, after all, giving grounds
for an insurrection. The realization in the world of these
ideas was new[14] : innovations in the political sphere,
which were yet conceived as *atemporal*, always true
and ever desirable; contemporaneous, if you like, with
homo sapiens. That is, innate. Grand and grave as these
principles were, the document, as a call to critical action,
was written in a hurry (though the rhetoric was carefully
revised). And that puts the latter-day armchair reader, as
opposed to the prospective revolutionary, in the strained

position of reading closely and critically what the rebel-to-be was to receive in an aroused and susceptible frame of mind. The justification for this skewed approach is both generally true for any published matter: once the author sends it forth, it casts loose from him; he can explain from now till doomsday, but it says what it says. And, in particular, if the document turns out to achieve world-historical standing, it becomes scripture of a kind, and every jot and tittle matters. I add here that I am truly perplexed about the author's writing. Were he Lincoln, my confident hypothesis would be that he always knew what *he* meant to say; not here: Jefferson sometimes, I think, let phrases take over.

That he had got hold of the American mind, at least in one aspect, seems to be true. Tocqueville, who was theologically drawn to America as the first great expression of God's Providence and socially somewhat repelled by its modeling a world of egalitarian mores, observed in Americans an "ardent" love of equality.[15]

Now equality, it is easy to see, is indeed in some

respects a human good (see Note 15). People, it hardly needs saying, are complexly different in themselves and on top of that complexly different from each other. Just one example from experience that I can't resist. There's nothing like the sweetness of austere persons or the malice of suave ones; yet until we learn otherwise, it is humanly right to accord them equal respect, as if they weren't worlds apart in bearability.

Now the moment might seem to have come to try to say what equality, in essence, *is*. Yet I want to hold off from this endeavor, which will inevitably seem "abstract"—though what could be more about dense being, more concrete, than an attempt to set out essence? I'll spend some more pages on appearances of equality in life, language, and soul—call it a sporadic, somewhat erratic phenomenology, the study of *"experience in human consciousness"*—a helpful though redundant phrase, since where else would experience take place?

To reiterate my aim: Equality is conceivable as a good-in-itself. I cannot believe that it actually is and will try to make a case for a human alternative. But first a moment's retrospection.

From the ancients we inherit the understanding of a human being as the only animal having articulable reason (*logos*).[16] In modern times that is replaced (among the equalizers) by the claim that to be human is to think of oneself as a being who is equal to other human beings, an opinion certainly not widespread in the rest of the animal kingdom, where dominance is the *modus vivendi*. Here too the question, "Whence our equality?" and its answer, "From God," is replaced by the question "What is equality?" on the reasonable hypothesis that the self-evidence—if indeed in the Declaration it is meant to apply across the leading sentence, and first to the existence of a Creator—is meant as well to cover the fact of equality. Then 1. self-evidently we are created and have a Creator who has endowed us, and 2. has endowed us with equality. It follows that equality must now become our question.

But a couple of preliminaries: Probably every competent adult would agree that we are all somatically endowed with physical hearts, blood-pumps. But probably there are quite a few Americans who are not ardent in the love of equality that Tocqueville ascribes to them (see Note 15), but whose self-sentiment tends more toward an inviolable individual worth that demands respectful recognition from the other human beings, even from those who are *not* equally endowed. Such souls are often not "sensitive," indeed a certain self-concentrated obtuseness may belong to their psychic make-up.

But if they are thoughtful in their self-segregation, their apartness from Tocqueville's democratic crowd, they may have balked at two words in the vocabulary of virtuous populists—among whom I count Lincoln who said somewhere that "God must have loved the common people; he made so many of them." So "common" is one word, and the other is "ordinary."

A user might well feel the laceration of a serrated knife's edge of ambiguity in these words. Both have at once a high and a low meaning. *Common* means both "shared" and "vulgar"; *ordinary* means both "normal" and "undistinguished."[17] This ambivalence corroborates my perplexity concerning the hairbreadth's divide between standard-adhering, thus elevated, commonality and debasing, indiscriminate tawdriness. Perhaps, above all, the word *discrimination,* which once meant social savvy and now means a social sin, makes the point. Thus, as our common, unearned dignity derives from our participation in a common species, the "wise kind," so we also share in its debasement, in the down-stretching gravity of our nature.[18] Similarly, we merit respect for submitting to personal and civic orderly ordinariness, for doing the expected, for joining the human work without therefore being undistinctive and undistinguished. In other words, there is a mediocracy that ranks as plain human. In fact, language itself reminds us: our forebears-in-speech sensed that even words used to convey distinction and dignity, words in which inequality lurks, can immediately flip into equality, our common de-distinguishing lot, as Nietzsche so repellently puts it, our lot as "herd-animals."[19] But never mind him. If our dignity is species-connate, nobody can, as they say, "give" anyone their dignity—or take it from them, except they themselves.

Now to turn back from word-meanings to the sentiments and thoughts coagulated in them. I must conjecture what dispositions really drive ardent lovers of equality (because how else would I know), perhaps even least from what they, probably not the most introspective lot, have averred.[20]

This equality-for-its-own-sake, I must emphasize, is really not primarily political. Or, when it is, it can co-exist, in fact be a condition of, tyranny. Herodotus tells a paradigmatic story: A young tyrant asks a more experienced one for advice on how to rule safely and nobly. The elder takes him on a silent walk through a wheat field and lops off all the tallest and finest ears. The younger man gets it: Equalize! He is taking Frost's equalizer tablet, though not to quiet the poor but to eliminate rivals. This is the worst of equalizations: the elimination of distinction, equalization for the sake of the worst of the equalities, that of one-over-many: tyranny.[21] This leveling sets at naught the Declaration. It subordinates to pervasive equality the "enough" that sustains life, the "sufficient" that enables liberty, and the "adequate" that underwrites the "pursuit" of happiness.

I might add a second thought to this view. Equalization to take down outstanding potential rivals, the equality of tyrannical suppression, has a nobly antithetical complement. There is an elevating equalization in the face of greatness. *Sub specie aeternitatis,* "under the aspect of eternity," we are all too diminutive to differ in stature. The noble response is reverence, of which more below. This equality-under-greatness has a very desirable pedagogic consequence, much to be welcomed by teachers: put a work of greatness before a class or a reading group, and the members can converse with each other without the inhibiting presumption of expert mastery or special experience. To be sure, the Declaration, whose body is a recitation of royal wrongs, is not the best example of greatness (but of efficacy). Then take another document, self-dated as spoken: "Four score and seven years ago" from the Declaration (1776 + 87 = 1863) and referencing its message, namely that the new nation was "conceived in," impregnated by, "our fathers," the Founders, in the marriage bed of Liberty and Life "dedicated to," that is, covenanted to "the proposition that all men are created equal"—Lincoln's *Gettysburg Address*, incomparable in subtlety of style conveying simplicity of feeling.[22]

Then what might be the attraction of equality as its own end? Is there an egalitarian temperament? Possibly; at least there might be age groups and individual moments when the nerve-wracking comparative mood is often upon us. This egalitarian disposition is the very inverse of that regard, that consideration which is the essence of respect. It is a squint-eyed peering, not for the sake of looking at, taking in, others, but of holding them off for inspection, so as to perform an assessment. It is *envy*.[23]

As so often, the etymology is revealing. Envy derives from the Latin verb *invidere*, "to look *into*, to examine closely"—invidiously. There can be, however, quite different motivations for looking. When Leeuwenhoek, in 1668, first applied his newly invented microscope to nature, a hitherto hidden world gained visibility, a source of delighted *and* appalled amazement—an ambivalence that Swift's Gulliver half-suppresses with comical innuendo in his account of those "little-thinkers," the Lilliputians (1726).

On the other hand, there is the intentness of lovers who cannot get their fill of looking—if they must, from a distance, if they can, ever-closer until looking is foreclosed. That is gazing—the world itself calls up an ocular grazing, a gratification of the eye. But there is also negative staring—hostile looking, often, envy. It is not, however, so much frank aggression as ambushing animosity. It is the egalitarian vice, less the sociable desire to establish equality than the sour wish to eliminate inequality.

Since equality and inequality are matters for calculating, and envy is engaged in very minute such figurings, the latter is, one might say, an unemotional passion.[24] Even if it seems to be ardently present, its fulfillment—equalization—leaves no resonance, no attachment. It is an arid satisfaction; if anything, it's succeeded by a next impulse to look for disparity, the next disadvantage. Therefore it needs a borrowed, adjuvant feeling, and that is *resentment*. Resentment, "anti-feeling," is an internally reactionary emotion.

So, far from being assuaged by a protuberance shaved off or a depression filled in, resentment then goes to minding the "patronizing" leveler of the field. But hold it! Am I shadowboxing here? *Are* there actually believers in mere equality who are in fact activated by this faith, who dwell in the wasteland of a made-up mind? The passionate animosity of a man who cannot himself be accused of a reactionary temperament, Nietzsche again, confirms to me the more than political, the personal potency of the egalitarian faith. He speaks of the terrible consequences of equality, the loss of all ranking order. This loss of "degree" (as Ulysses would say: see Note 21) accords to everyone, Nietzsche says, the right to every problem—for he knows that the power to pose the problem, to frame the agenda, is a primary public capability. In sum, he condemns the egalitarian faith as "the superstition of the 'equal human being'."[25]

That's testimony to the deleterious power of the egalitarian idea from two centuries back, and one more century back would bring us to an initial virulent event in the worldly playing out of a still very active rivalry between the conceptual pair of Liberty and Equality—the decade of the French Revolution (1789–99). This event was a testament to the fact that there is no learning from history, because the American Revolution (1776), nearly a generation earlier, was simply more wisely conducted in respect to the crucial protection of Liberty from Equalization. By visions grand enough to encompass them, the safe and sane relation of Liberty and Equality then enunciated and reiterated later in the *Gettysburg Address*, cited above, were actualized on the American continent.

IS EQUALITY AN ABSOLUTE GOOD?

Nonetheless, there are fellow citizens to whom equality, in Lincoln's understanding the somewhat secondary notion, is a more heartfelt concern, not only as a policy matter but as a way of life, socially and personally. They could more easily bear to see a diminution in our freedoms and our liberty than a growth in inequality. Curing inequality, however, which is in little and in large respects pervasive under personal freedom enabled by political liberty, means undertaking, or rather attempting to bring about, "systemic reform," that is, administratively led revolution.

Moreover, it's often done in a rush to action, without a concrete vision of the substantive positive good, beyond the correction of a relational flaw, that is to be achieved. Nor are the pitfalls of systemic correction, those "unintended consequences," concretely imagined—because hurry quashes the imagination, whose good work is tentative, diffuse, and leisurely (interspersed by hard-edged, dense, and sudden episodes). Perhaps the chief conceptual inadequacy is the assumption that there *is* a system. To me, a system is a contrivance such that, if you throw a lever here, something reliable happens there. By that criterion we don't live in a system but amidst a heap of mutually interfering semi-systems. It works tolerably well, and—a blessing—it's not amenable to sudden reform, not to mention the fact that some of its most zealous, busiest would-be agent-provocateurs have a positive talent for negative results. Thus incremental improvements without much discombobulation and reversible innovations before much ineradicable damage seem best to me.

There are other difficulties in the way of successful equalizations, chief of them the recalcitrances of the unideologized human heart. For example, once the fulfillment of an essentially negative desire like the leveling of inequalities has been achieved, what now? The event, instead of being followed by the exhilaration of gained success, is followed by the lethargy of a lost cause: Though the inequality is leveled out, the goals are redistributed, we each have a (very little) bit more—and we couldn't care less, for the good causes that stimulated our souls, being gained, are gone. Not even *Schadenfreude,* the "joy-in-another's-harm," is logically operative: Hadn't we claimed that being equal (and so, being equalized) is a supervening delight?

Further: Ardent equalizers are sometimes gripped by an ideological zealotry that drives out all secular reverence.[26] That phrase is not a contradiction in terms; I mean this somewhat awed, occasionally acute, awareness that there is an, if imperfectly, surveyable World hosting a Nature and its natures at least partially accessible to my understanding—accessible to my species, and, as far as I've heard, to none other. This faith-comparable but not necessarily religious feeling includes in its sphere the mundane, the ordinary, and the common.

Sometimes it seems that this very fact of our species-superiority should be enough to satiate our not easily suppressible desire to be *someone's* superior, our native inegalitarianism. Not so incidentally, this somewhat pernicious longing turns out to be the basis of our betterment: We learn that outshining *others* is a mean and idle pleasure, and we invert the usual sense, "out-rising" others, and rise above ourselves, become our own betters: self-inequality, so to speak.

Reverence, it will be no surprise, is yet another "looking" word. In its Latin origin it means a guarding, watching, awareness. As envy functions where equality is desired, so reverence applies when inequality is accepted. For, once more, equalization overlooks degree of quality in its items in favor of quantitative leveling. Even when, in order to justify a judgment of equality, we say that two things or people are of equal quality, we have imposed a ratable aspect on them and now regard them quantitatively. I see that procedure as practically always illegitimate. Being a teacher, grading comes first to my mind: "This student" (why is the student graded, why not rather the essay, demonstration, report?) "gets" (is it a benefaction?) "a B, that one a B-." What possible sense can this make? One wrote a spirited rant, the other produced a pedantic analysis. What power am I giving the grade letters, really crypto-numbers, to make the in-comparable equal or, by half a grade, unequal?

Strange as it seems, I shall argue below that equality is essentially quantitative, while inequality is essential-ly qualitative. Had these two students submitted identi-cal essays (it happened once at my college, though over a decade apart: the same senior essay on Kant; we re-scinded the later degree) they would have, unproblem-atically, gotten an equal grade, since every quantifiable feature would have been identical. And it would have been a B because the quality was good and, it turns out, B also means "good"—less than A, "excellent," better than C, "mediocre." The qualitative sense is attached to the (hidden) numbers by a metaphor of ordinality, A, the initial letter of the alphabet means "first," or "best"; B means "second-best," so "merely good."

In sum, while equality de-qualifies objects or people, reverence does the reverse: Equality squishes groups into masses, quashing individuality, while reverence converts gatherings into congregations, elevating the soul.

I'll add one more deleterious effect on the soul of a devotion to equality as an absolute good. It is the psychic training already mentioned, of disregarding substance for relation. The blatant example is the phrase currently most used to refer to a primary but unofficial personal attachment: "to be in a relationship."[27] "Be in," logically speaking, must mean "to have the role of a term in a relation," but it is the relation that is named, *is made substantial*, nominal. Its *termini,* the lovers, are suppressed. The less with-it writers of graffiti still say "Joe loves Jill," which begins and ends with a boy and a girl and has a feeling in the middle. It is, however, not direction-neutral, as is "in a relationship," but gives the declarative initiative to one, usually the male. And that may be why the middle-class young are in relationships: "Nick wishes to be in a relationship with Norma" is not seductive, while the phrase in question projects a *fait accompli* without a lead-term.

Equality is surely, strictly speaking, a mere relation, and that must, I imagine, affect its terms, people. Being equal is not an endowment like a gift, a talent, say being musical. One reading of the Declaration, given above, does stipulate, however, that we have the right to life, liberty, and happiness by reason of our equality, that they are somehow *grounded in equality*. Yet another reading, also set out above, claims that our aboriginal equality has no connection to this three-pronged endowment, and that these rights are gifts from the Creator quite separate from our equal creation. To me, it would, on this reading, be permissible to consider that we have these rights in very unequal degree: Some are sturdier in body than others; some know better what to do with their opportunities than others; some know better how to find reliable enjoyment than others.

Once more: Being equal has no concrete positive consequences. Its good begins and ends when you have what everyone else has, which, for purposes of equal assignment has to be more or less of the same sort: de-qualified and, instead, quantified. So being equal is not being, say, musical, or being educated, which brings articulable benefits.[28] In fact, the alert egalitarian, while on the lookout for inequalities, will often overlook, even ruin, a going good. Life and fiction abound in stories of children and supposed adults, who, embroiled over equal distribution, end up with the goods in question despoiled. Especially in children, equality-battles can be as numerous as possession-battles.

These internecine quarrels are local, and political programs for repairing inequality are not very effective, so both are self-limiting. But the passion bent on eradicating inequality from our moral framework flares into virulence now and then and finds us vulnerable. Goods are taken away, and some are much poorer while some are much wealthier.

But before turning to some modest proposals, I must repair the omission of a task that is, I think, always crucial in an attempt to get insight into, and a handle on, a practical problem caused by a notional defect: I should try to say what equality as an idea is, give some exposition that is not a definition but a circumscription of the meaning behind the term. No more is it an "abstraction" (as people are apt to call dealings with ideas), because nothing is *less abstracted*, "drawn off," its substance than an idea; indeed, ideas are the most densely concrete objects if not in, then out of, our world.[29]

So here is an attempt to answer the question: What, in essence, in its very being, is Equality? The word is derived from a Latin adjective *aequus*, which bears in it the notion of "leveling." A primary sense, still lurking in equality, is spatial; in the plain of a landscape no hills or hollows, in the plane of geometry no break-outs into the solid dimension—evenness.

I don't know if it is determinable whether equality was first a moral term connoting fairness or a mathematical term denoting level quantity. In any case, it is indispensable to both arithmetic and geometry, so basic that no book on my mathematical shelves bothers to define it. In determining the equality of two numbers the levelling notion works: Starting with the first one, stack them each in ordinal fashion in two columns next to each other, and if they end up with the tops level, the numbers are equal.

In geometric figures (for simplicity, of plane geometry) the equality looked for is area. Figures are congruent or similar rather than equal or unequal. They have outlines or circumferences, and these do have lengths comparable in size. Those lengths may change considerably in transformation, which, however, leave the areas the same. For example, put a square between two parallel lines which act as rails, so to speak, and pull the top side of the square along the top rail; the sides are thought of as extensible, will get longer and longer, as long as you like, as the square is transformed into the type of parallelogram called "rhombus," the *area will remain equal*, as Euclid proves (Book I, Proposition 36). Similarly for the so-called Pythagorean theorem: The two squares on the short sides of a right triangle are transformed, disappear into the larger square built on the triangle's hypotenuse, which now contains exactly the areas of the smaller squares added to each other. This equality of area under transformation of shape suggests that area has some qualities of matter, like a lump of dough that can be rolled out and cut up into various figures and then kneaded back into a ball. This strange fact prompted the Neoplatonist Plotinus to introduce the hybrid notion of "mathematical matter," a thought-dough that *retains its size within different shapes*.[30] Thus equality, so lucid for numbers, enters geometry through the mysterious intelligible materiality of area. But perhaps it's not so strange. Geometry, after all, is done in the imagination, which is closer to the constituents of perception—among which is matter— than is the pure intellect.

This, then, is Equality:

It is, first, a relation between two, or among several terms, hence nothing is in itself equal or endowed with equality as a quality; it is, second, relative, since the relation of equality is discerned by comparison; it is, third, determinate, unique, for a given case, while its antithetical complement, inequality, has indeterminably many instances; it is, fourth, as a relation a sort of sameness, sameness not in the casual use of "simply identical," but more accurately, of "imperfect identity," identity that has enough difference not to collapse the relation into unity; equality is, fifth, applicable over a variety of venues, to mathematical objects as quantity (multitude and magnitude), a primary use; to the perceptual world as quality (properties); to the merit-dispensing sphere as degree (rank); in the moral realm as wages (of sin).

This, so smoothly current notion, engages, so to speak, in strangely recalcitrant shenanigans once it is taken at its word. In sum, equality as defective identity owes its relationality to this defect: perfect identity is self-involved, imperfect identity harbors difference, so gives birth to relationality. But equality itself contributes the terms, so to speak: What is to be equalized are usually material things, but above all sapient humans.[31]

There's more to say about inordinate inequality, which needs to be acknowledged when I am claiming inequality as a political and personal good. Not that I mean to repeat here the litany against material greed and showy excess. It goes without saying that these warnings are righteous, and I've written them out only because the obvious needs reiterating so as not to cease to be obvious—because these American commonplaces are predominantly sound.

They do, however, imply a question: How, if at all, is inequality related to fairness, to just rewards for out-standing effort? Do the best off have an argument?

Here my experience fails, and I must resort to imagination. So I suppose that, from the vantage of one who is sitting on billions, your fellow citizens fall into two equal castes—your fellow billionaires, a tiny group of competing equals, and the others at large, who all look much the same; living in an alien or forgotten world of small doings, almost a different caste.[32] This second set of equals-to-each-other-but-not-to-you are oddly closer to you than your fellow billionaires, since they lay out your tuxedo, serve your canapés, and bring up your children. With both of these two-tiered, contradictory equalities, social intercourse is with all good will (and prudence) highly fraught. The ugly ultimate in this aberrant equality is the regime of the one-over-many.

Its modern form is a German *Führer* and his *Volk,* in antiquity, the tyrant and his *polis* and, most grandly, the Persian King of Kings and his motley nations. Herodotus draws a memorable psychological portrait of Xerxes, whose grandees are never safe from the fear of a sudden fall into hapless equality.[33]

As a complement to large generalities, however, I want to turn to the small and the particular, to the "confines of home"—a literal locution these months of pandemic lockdown. To be sure, my home is my castle and I its chatelaine. So I ask: Does managing my little domain involve some concern with equality?

Well, what doesn't? What life-agenda, what clock-watching, appointment-making, and, above all, getting down to work, can't be framed thus: Is this effort equal in worth to that? Isn't that satisfaction going to be very unequal to that pleasure of this indulgence? Here is an example.[34] If old age is fairly jocund, there is—clearly advance training for transit into non- or other-being— sleep, which commands more and more of the day. Is it OK to leave the world to its own devices for more than half, for an unequally divided day?

Life at large tends to have a certain sweep; one thing leads to another; every deed involves more doing. But at home most activities are self-limiting, though never done for good. The lintel of my study door is going out of whack, so I get my little plane and hone away; the picture of a dear, dead friend has gone askew; do I get up to rectify it—him? Or do I go on scribbling, these so minute physical actions that assume so great a consequence, these graphite offspring (which I wouldn't dream of "processing")? All-in-all home is a place of mundane sweetness, where equanimity of mind betokens that ultimate equality of small things: a score of urgencies—and nothing much matters, really. Enough exemplifying detail; on to a final, a practical question.

What part of our soul will we call on to extract

ourselves from an unworthy devotion to equality and a candid acknowledgement that it is not un-American to cherish inequality—that it might, in fact, make our daily conduct more warmly—not egalitarian, but respectful, regardful: a communion of incommensurables.[35]

I say "our," because few Americans are not sometimes in their hearts believers in equality pure and simple. Can there be an affection for Americans being American, *en masse*—as if a crowd could have a face? Most of us wouldn't go as far as does Friedrich Schiller's "Ode to Joy" (the text of the last movement of Beethoven's Ninth). Poetry should usually be visualized; this had better not be; unless you're in a very Whitmanesque mood, it's somewhat off-putting:

> *Seid umschlungen Millionen!*
> *Diesen Kuss der ganzen Welt!*

> Be embraced, you Millions!
> This kiss to the whole world!

Yuck! No, just affectionate, pictorially enhanced patriotism will do; and yes, there are sometimes accesses of generic love—a contradiction in terms, to be sure, because love is particular. But then, there are also self-contradictory feelings.

This, then, is my blessedly unoriginal—and even less, "creative"—answer to the question: Where, within ourselves, do we look to defang moral egalitarianism? *It is our will* or free will. The latter phrase is actually redundant, useful only before we've agreed that the will, rightly understood as our agent-power, is, by its very meaning, free. An unfree will is one vitiated by either extreme: weak will down to submissive will-lessness or willfulness up to dominating self-assertion.[36]

The classical mainstream understanding of the will is remarkable, conceptually and experientially. The will is both at once: rational desire *and* desirous reason.[37] Our affective capability for passionate wanting and our intellectual faculty for rational thinking are mutually inclusive. That means they are identical when counted, namely one, but distinguishable in understanding, thus two. We can see ourselves as primarily emotional beings; enraptured, ravished, captivated; yet we are the while also observing, calculating, even cunning beings. Thus poetry is among the most intellectually demanding activities, yet some great poetry is written by lovers, testimony to the compatibility of passion and intellect—indeed, their mutual embrace. From the other aspect, the very name for an often sensation-devoid inquiry, philosophy, the *love* of wisdom, is a testimonial to the eros-cognate feel of all sorts of inquiry—not only philosophy, to which analogy two major Platonic dialogues, the *Phaedrus* and the *Symposium,* are devoted, but also research of all sorts, from detective work to laboratory experiments—whose devotees exhibit some symptoms seen in love; they can't stay away from the venue, office or laboratory, especially at night, when the object of their pursuit will, if ever, make an appearance.

So the will in the classical understanding is not a sudden seizure or impulse—which implies that willing as an extended engagement takes time—the temporality of the slow, lingering eroticism of thoughtful inquiry.

It is a staged—Thomas detailed it—but not a jigged process of exploration, conceiving possibilities and coming to a culmination, a conclusion: the readiness to do, the technical vocabulary speaks of the decision to "execute," to act.[38] And it really works more or less like that, as people know who've been in the hot seat of decision that demands coolth of the head and urgency of the blood. A waffling will is apt to go ineptly sodden, as a forcible will goes dangerously deaf.

Finally, the sound will is not austerely driven—daydreaming, snacks, fugue states, naps belong to its temporality. It all ends with the understated, consequential, "I've been thinking this over…"

And because we're somewhat the wiser for working through this classical willing, we're more protected against the curious agentless malice of those "unintended consequences."[39]

So I can marshal this slow but determined will against another will-defect; sitting, fidgeting on a moral picket fence and being to others a pain where the fence hurts. I am passing here from civic and political freedom, in my terms, from liberty, to affective and intellectual freedom simply—in short, from outer to inner freedom, where the will is at home. Recall that I am trying to show that it is the will that can save us from mistaken mantras.

I haven't so far referenced actual cases, so here's one that can stand for all. CNN, January 31, 2021, commentator's thrown-off phrase: "…the kind of economic equality we're all looking for."

So, not all. I'm just listening to one of my best-loved Bach cantatas (BMV 176). "There is something defiant yet timorous about the heart of all human beings." (Jeremiah, Luther Bible: "*Es ist das Herz ein trotzig und verzagt Ding; wer kann es ergründen?*—"Who can get to its bottom?" For Bach the defiance predominates— the music is pulsingly, exhilaratingly "defiant" and the word is sung over and over by the chorus; "timorous" or "despairing" is outsung.

The will, of course, drives exterior activities, from the inside out. It is in charge of those we call "conduct," not of "behavior," which is impulsive or habitual—re-active, mostly.[40] I think I can find, through this inward turn, a way out of the egalitarian fixation which is quite distinct from the voguish "linguistic turn" of the last century.[41] What is wanted is a human capacity that effectuates notions of togetherness in us which don't require an almost-identity, a sameness, but, on the contrary, individual incommensurability.

Why is the will that recourse? In its wayward course as will-lessness or will-fulness, it can wreak havoc. But when sound, it is the very locus of our individuality. It is at once all our particular own and all a common human endowment. Here meet and merge the two great roots of our soul, awareness and its first great consequence, love: thought and desire. Where these show themselves as mutually comprehending, there our circumstantial disparities disappear. The specimens of other animals are more alike from birth than human individuals.[42] Yet the more we grow from *infants*—non-talkers, into animals having actual *logos*, rational speech, the more distinctive we become *just as* we become more generically human—which is the second reason why we like to talk to each other, the first one being that we like to hear ourselves being heard.

The classical will is central to this inquiry precisely in this version: First, judgment, evident in discerning openness to good objects, and then cleverly deliberate choice of means, are comprehended in this capability.[43]

One first delivery of our judgment ought to be that inordinate inequality may lead (for articulable reasons I've begun to mention) to the exercise of unauthorized power and thus become deleterious to the body politic. Nonetheless, while conditions of liberty equalize us as citizens, releasing the inborn inequality of our gifts and furthering the cultivation of our possibilities, particularly our acquisitive powers, they do cause inequality among us as private persons. I would argue that as long as these excesses of disparity are compatible with universal sufficiency, we should teach ourselves to live with them. That is a hard lesson for true believers in equality; it is overlooking a moral offense. But too zealous attempts to rectify natural outcomes fail, and leave bad blood.

But to return to our will as a respectable source of a decent inequality—by its very essence. "Will," a noun, is an almost-homonym with "will," an inflected form of the verb "to be," its future tense. I say "almost" because a homonym is a word that looks exactly like another word but has a different meaning. Now, the noun "will" is a capability and the verb "to be" denotes a state, so they don't have the same meaning, except that both do refer to the future. I'll put a brief attempt at recording the ins and outs of this pair in a note.[44] But this aspect of the will as future-directed needs a word here: In this capacity the will has recourse to our imaginative faculty. The imagination works by employing time to overcome time; it uses memory-images from lived bygone experiences, or from lettered learning, or even from vision-seeking excursions into the hinterland of consciousness where live the imagination's prototypes (about which I inquire in my book *Feigning*). For since to will means to determine the mere, blank future into concreteness by outfitting it with vivid views, the imagination must go to work. It may resort to its memory-store of once-real scenes or supply its own imaginary images, which are quasi-bygone as well: "Once upon a time."[45] In any case, the imagination brings the past into the future, where it wears a new costume. Thus the future will gain substance for its otherwise unsubstantiated mere intentions. For, in sum, the will is all these; it is mere intention: pure futurity; it is executive intention: decision-making; it is judging intention: choice-making; it is perception-invoking: imagination-summoning.

This will will, when sound and held to account, *favor inequality*. For though it can order up a measurement (I will speak of it as the actor, but I mean me, you) it is not itself measurable. It is non-metric as being us, our unextended, unique crux. The will's inclination toward inequality follows from its being beyond measurement.

I mean this as consequential: No one, least of all a psychometrician, can know another's will, unless it is dispersed into its abnormalities. The problem of insight is compounded here. The will is under the governance of reason, which is—who can tell?—either the most law-bound or the most spontaneous of agencies. And the will is also desire, which is the most impulsive and the most ineradicable of passions. Add that its fruition, its execution, is highly circumstantial. So even long and intimate knowledge sets you up for a surprise. Above all, as Heraclitus says: "Nature loves to hide herself."[46]

The practical consequences of our inability to measure human being (partly because we cannot define our essence extensively, that is, as a topography with defined borders and territory to be surveyed) become serious especially in supposedly radical egalitarian revolutions, where a country's whole wealth, including its real estate, are up for reassignment. Simply equal division is never accepted as equitable, as fair. Since minds can be captured but not assessed, leaders have had recourse to totalitarian socialization; movements with pre-composed mantras, organized protests against offenses not experienced by participants, rallies with speeches at once inciting and benumbing. The object for those behind the scenes is to reduce the human multitude to a mass, where persons lose their incomparable individual being to become subjects for quantification, either as mere numbers (usually dishonestly estimated) or as human dough, psychologically malleable.[47]

So precisely because the will is not measurable, I claim it is inclined toward inequality. That is because equality is more metric than inequality. Here is what I mean:

The famous first sentence of Tolstoy's *Anna Karenina* reads: "All happy families are alike; each unhappy family is unhappy in its own way." This only modestly true dictum in our day of deliberate diversity can be turned inside out to a truth about equals and unequals: "All egalitarian societies are the same; each inegalitarian society is unequal in its own way."

To determine the equality of two or more beings you must find a common measure by which to "compare" them; the word means what it says: It puts items together, "on par," it finds if they are equal (par = equal). And that requires that they be commensurable, have a common measure that can be applied to them separately. (Of course, some items are such that you can simply apply them to each other without a mediating measure, as two friends measure their heights directly by standing back to back against each other.)

If the results are negative, the beings are unequal. There are surely more unequals than equals on our earth, a good thing because equals are more demanding, measurewise, than unequals. You might indeed say equals are more metric than unequals.[48] For unequals, the multitudes on either side of the unique, precise equals can be as incommensurable as you like. Beyond the first few minimals, you can eyeball inequality; you needn't measure it to enunciate it. So inequality might be thought of as less measure-needy, more metrically relaxed—until you go into inordinate excess and exact measurement becomes a tool for advocating equalization and "How much more?" matters.

It is surely significant that equality is the positive condition, definite and unique, while inequality, indeterminate and infinite, is negative—as are all its synonyms, it seems: unequal, disparate, uneven, different (*dis* = not, apart).

Lovers of equality think, I imagine, that universal equalization would simplify life because it eliminates differences. But that's a misapprehension. Since equality is absolutely precise, small deviations are all too apparent, so that well-known animosity, resentment over small differences, surges; irritation becomes a way of life, the envious life mentioned above. If you're long on ideology, you're apt to be short on humanity; "-ists," for example feminists, may decry womanliness.

That is how the will, always on the side of freedom, becomes the partisan of inequality: Inequality means latitude in possibility, escape from comparison, release from positive definition—all preconditions of lived freedom. And the will prefers, nay *is* our freedom. Hence it is the aboriginal inegalitarian when most itself.

"Itself"—"I, myself"—to think of the will, *my* will, is to think of selfhood. What is a self? It is always, it appears, to think of a *person*, for only persons can be agents. Perhaps that's backwards. Not persons only are agents, but any agent must show signs of personhood, as I've laid it out: be a unique individuality under the aegis of communality; be *sui generis,* "in a class by him/herself" *while* being a species-being, *homo sapiens*[49]—or a *res imaginaria,* an "imaginary thing."

And it can't be said often enough that the soul in its soundly happy activity, what Aristotle calls *energeia* and *eudaimonia*—the soul being at its own work and doing it well—is way beyond measurement. Happiness indices belong to a litter I think of as idiots' expertise. It's not a problem of incommensurability and its irrationality—a mathematical problem.[50] It is rather, once more, that, seen from one point of view, the will lacks what's needed for quantification (magnitude and multitude, extension and countability), but from another that it has what it takes to be a Self: *reflexivity, that is, self-comprehension.* So my will is both I and Me—and a constitutional inegalitarian. As if to corroborate the aboriginality of the human will, there is that spectacular, just post-infancy episode known as the "Terrible Twos."[51]

Here is the first stanza of a song, probably meant to be somewhat subversive, that German children learned. It is worth citing and caviling with, since, although it means to assert human independence, it does it on will-less grounds:

> *Thoughts are free, who can guess them?*
> *They flit by like nocturnal shadows.*
> *No human being can know them, no hunter*
> *   shoot them*
> *So once and for all: Thoughts are free.*[52]

We sang it in the mid-thirties; the Nazis had just established themselves in power; Jews were about to be deported to extermination camps. This so innocent song cannot be blamed for, but *is* explanatory of, the meager, albeit heroic, German resistance. Internality, the venue for silent thought, is surely the enabler of privacy, but how can it be the cause of freedom? Secrecy can protect, but it can as easily frustrate freedom. For willing culminates in ordering an action, and acting means relinquishing life as a private person (for whom the Greek word is *idiotes*) and going public, in fact often, publishing. Moreover, if thoughts flit about like blind bats, they cannot *ipso facto* be free. Perhaps the thoughts of Freethinkers are like that, but are not all of us, insofar as we are genuinely trying, Boundthinkers? In mutual embrace with desire, thoughts make us free and unequal because they are afflicted (or blest) with this perennial problem: the deep question whether thinking is *bound by the truth,* as desire is *engaged to the beauty of its object.* I might even say that this is the gravity of thinking, its ponderousness—that, insofar as it is free, it seeks bondage—seeks to be bound by truth's necessity. But above all, secrecy belongs in this register of what I might call the circumstantialities of thinking, as a willed withholding of something suspected of attracting curiosity. Opaqueness is *not* the business of that in us which brings us from the theoretical into the practical life. There are, of course, the confidentialities of tact and harm-suppression, not of self- but of other-protection. These are ruled by the secret of secrets: Nobody should know that there *is* a secret.

No, the will is utterly non-opaque, absolutely self-transparent. I mean by that: This function knows not only what it is up to but why and how; above all, it knows that it doesn't know—most of what others know and nothing of what nobody else knows. This knowledge descends to the will from its *being* Thought, Intellect. It bears on the will's leaning toward inequality by enforcing on our consciousness—for self-consciousness is at its most poignantly comprehensive in willing—the basic inequity, the blessed unfairness of life's assignments of comforts and dis-eases.

Interim summary: It is not opacity that makes us free, as the song wrongly sings, but openness; flexible staunchness in absorbing newness without succumbing to the sterile siren's song of *novelty*—a substance-deprived formality *similar in this substancelessness to equality*.[53] Or to protecting traditional treasure very ardently without denying that living later has its advantages.

It follows, incidentally, that if these attempts to describe inner freedom make sense, then a current exhortation by equalizers doesn't: We're to "give people their dignity." You can get a coach for demure demeanor, but no one can bestow dignity of the soul because that's us, being all there, fully human and fully us. Consequently, there may be people who have no dignity. Here the principle of "ignorance acknowledged" goes to work: We don't know who they are, and nobody is rightfully deprived of their right to have rights (in retrospect, by one interpretation of the Declaration that right to rights came precisely from our equal creation).

To conclude: The reply to my titular question, "Is Equality an Absolute Good?" is *No*. Now, with a little more assurance, the answer is "It's sometimes a good but never good-in-itself."

And here is a postlude, a return from an imagined political intervention to a present philosophical concern, since after sixty-four years at my school, I have persuaded myself that *every* screed should end, return to, a question to go on with, for good.

Equality is imperfect sameness, sameness is imperfect identity. Both equality and sameness are, if relations can be said to have an essence, essentially relations: you can't be same or equal on your own. Identity is a condition regarded as a relation: self-sameness.[54] You can be identical on your own, namely to yourself. It's a derivative possibility, stemming from our ability to fall interestingly sick: self-alienation. "Imperfect" means lacking some property that keeps you from being totally something set up as a model. Thus sameness needs an other to operate, whereas identity is whole in itself. And equality is not sameness in every possible respect but mainly in quantity, quantity either in some way that is essentially quantitative such as money or commodities, or quality that is, for this purpose, metaphorically attributed quantitatively, such as dignity or excellence. Thus: identity > sameness > equality, more forceful, that is, in achieving unification.

There is also, besides increase, a mutual relation these terms have to each other—each to all: *similarity*. I think similarity is one of the most interesting notions comprising our mental stock. Here is why and how similarity matters, as a last thought bearing on a preference for inequality.

Similarity is at home in geometry with perfect clarity. It is involved with all the most interesting and consequential notions of elementary geometry: the theory of proportion, parallelism, areal measurement (as set out above), and, above all, the consequent possibility: figures that have the same shape but differ in size.[55]

This last, geometrically formalizable, possibility pervades our lives, since on it depends the making of images. But again, that's putting the cart before the horse: We, the hominids, are image-makers from early on.[56] That is not, of course, because geometry treats of similar figures but the converse: We are born imaging—I mean born with mental imagery, and so there is, eventually, a theory of similarity—definitions, axioms, proof-patterns. Think who we would be if figures could not preserve shape under indefinitely many changes of size; imagine the size of our imagination-subserving brains if we were still able to imagine the solar system!

So from the geometric abstraction to the immattered world: Are not all discernibly different items of our environment similar as well, if only in being, though distinct, yet all items? Is an absolutely dissimilar thing even conceivable?—certainly *not* imaginable. Whence come criteria for no longer calling them comparable, similar, but pronouncing them incomparable—absolutely different?

These are not so-called academic questions, since the answers are humanly fraught. For example, how insistently can we emphasize difference, "diversity," before we are, with a shock, brought back to a bare basic truth about majoritarian democracy (and euphemistic dictators notwithstanding; Is there another kind?): Stripped to its foundations, divested of its expressive demeanors, it is colorlessly numerical. One vote more in a division of millions, and they govern, though barely; 4 million more, and they're less willing to compromise; 40 million more, it's a landslide, and they have a hard time controlling their extremists. All these outcomes, though pure nose-counting, are full of human affects—which can in turn be quantified: life—many years, liberty—many opportunities, happiness—much success.

Then the question arises: Given that equality, being a comparative and precisely determinable relation, requires hard, that is, quantitative assessment—is quantification an inescapable aspect of American democracy, of its hard, majoritarian heart? I think the answer is Yes. Am I retracting my aversion to equality and its zealous egalitarianism, now underwritten quantitatively? No, only qualifying it. For egalitarianism and its devotions do not need to follow.

Come election day, I walk to the polling place—a curiously composite being for the hour: *at once* a decision-maker, a being with a faculty of choice and execution, my will. And I am, as well, a unit, walking to add myself as a number to numbers. I enter, the rolls are checked, I pull a curtain and press levers on the machine or drop a ballot in a box, receive my "I voted" sticker, say hello to my neighbors and strut home, full of elated satisfaction, seized by a sort of mundane sacredness or worldly holiness: I'm a citizen—"naturalized" to boot: "Big as life and twice as natural."[57]

So for that civic holyday, the sense of felt equality is not degrading but proud. Nor is the equalizing that counteracts inordinate, unhealthy inequality—well, maybe not proud, but acceptable. Not so the equalizing equality; it debases dignity by its vices, envy and resentment, and it depresses enterprise by its discouragement of disparity.[58] In sum, such equality cannot be a positive good because it is primarily relative in its essence, called on more to depress ambition, inhibit enterprise, program redistribution, preach adjustment, than to support initiative, energy, production, spiritedness. I think of inequality as mirroring, in the realm of quantity, a characteristic of the human will: While internally as reason-bound as anything could be—for it is itself reason—it is, from the outside, untamable and reticent; it can't be second-guessed.

Although a thinking person might have a good chance, to an unreflective bystander its—the will's, the human being's—opinions, judgments, decisions may seem unpredictable, not because they are antic but because they are both "comprehending," large-scoped and summary, and "perspicacious," penetrating and interfused, both engaged in the commonalities that subserve individuality. It is, as the Germans say, our "ownmost" (*eigentlichste*) power.[59] It is the composite capacity of making up our minds (or better, letting our minds determine us) and determining our body to thought-informed behavior, to *conduct*. I think of the will as having this position in our life: The base of our being is in our affects, passions, feelings; our culmination is in musing, thinking, intuiting. And our engagement with our world is in judging, choosing, deciding—the will's particular work. It is not a capacity likely to be a partisan of imperfect identity—except insofar as it, the will itself, imposes this sameness—but on others, not on its own human host.

This speculation follows: How productive of some

practical good would it be if those who do the public talking tried to break themselves of habitual appeals for equality and went after "enough," after widespread sufficiency? For being equal is a very odd predicate for felicity, while the pursuit of happiness does require a sufficiency of means.[60] It is, however, blessedly impracticable to equalize "enough." For candor (which is better than occasional pretense and far better than habitual hypocrisy) demands acknowledging a difficult truth; "Enough" is not apportionable by some determinable number. For what expert, such as a social worker, can really judge the means for self-help, the special needs that an actual person has? Moreover, going from the generality of our ultimate ignorance concerning our fellow humans' affairs to an unwelcome local fact: Distribution of *sufficiency is rooted in inequality.* It is, to be sure, ideologically conceivable as restitution of some entitlement withheld or redistribution to level the playing field—as equalizations. But that masks the truth while adding nothing to the benefaction: Some are getting more, others less, on grounds that seem fair to some and not to others. For the "enough" with which I would wish us to replace "equal" is just *not* equalizable: What if you have a child that *needs* to own a violin and to learn from a really good teacher to play on it—say Bach's six sonatas for solo violin? *Very* expensive.

ADDENDUM

My colleague Joan Silver just gave me Elizabeth Marshall Thomas's *The Old Way* (2006), a non-ideological account of those ultimate egalitarians, the Bushmen of the Kalahari Desert. This people, whose culture is now extinct, had a tribal defect, jealousy. The avid desire for equality was their response to this vice. I see in this affect a corroboration for the main thesis of the above essay: Equality may quench envy even more effectively than would universal prosperity, were the latter universally distributed. But then, near-perfect equality might actually exacerbate the vice, and perfect equality make it ragingly endemic: all-round invidiousness.

ENDNOTES

1   Or its somewhat artful avoidance of them. In graduate school at Yale in the fifties a sort of reverse snobbery was practiced. It was a sign of newcomers' cluelessness to call your teacher "Professor." "Mr." was the coy style, and it was up to you to discern the academic rank order that assuredly obtained.

2   Of course, there are the ones who are full of founding energy; often they bring into being (and sadly see out of being) little schools with exuberantly imaginative or gravely classical curricula or small niche businesses such as have a complete inventory of soldiers in every uniform from horse-hair crested to steel helmet and carrying every small arm from bronze-tipped spear to Enfield rifle.

3   Outrage: When did it become a mark of virtue? It used to meet one's mother's response: "Calm down, and then we'll talk." Anyhow, being a recreation of the speech-encouraged privileged, it rarely leads to work-requiring engagement.

4   It hardly needs saying that this essay owes much to Alexis de Tocqueville's *Democracy in America* (1840), particularly to Vol. II, Pt. iv, Ch. 6, on what he had not yet a name for, but we call conformism. Tocqueville on the wealthy: Vol. I, Pt. ii, Ch. 2.

A book I received too late for inclusion uses exactly the same terms as I do: Deirdre Nansen McCloskey, *Bourgeois Equality: How Ideas, Not Capital or Institutions, Enrich the World* (2016).

The book on the dangers of great wealth, especially dubiously come by, is Francis Scott Key Fitzgerald's *The Great Gatsby* (1925), whose doomed hero is that most lovable of lovable bad boys (some of whom I've taught), Jay Gatsby himself. His etymology: *Gats*: "of a gun" (slang for pistol) plus *by*: "boy" (*Oxford English Dictionary*, see -by 2), so "son of a gun," or "hell of a kid"—as he was.

5   First Amendment: "Congress shall make no law…abridging the freedom of speech, or of the press…"

6   Happiness: Aristotle, *Nicomachean Ethics* 1098 a 14. I should say here that the word "soul," that principle of my motions, is not much in vogue in a present-day secular speech. As far as I'm concerned, people are welcome to disavow their souls and be soulless. I say, to misapply Galileo: "And yet it moves." Or they may prefer "consciousness," or even "brain." People, however, who think their brain thinks (rather than that it subserves thinking) are usually devoted to perceivable evidence, and no picture of a sliced brain that I've seen ever shows a thought as I experience it—as a non-sensory intentional activity, *almost* always accompanied by quasi-sensual imagery and by an affect of some sort. "Affect," incidentally is not, to me, a dynamic physical relation. We

do speak, metaphorically, of Sun and Earth being mutually attracted. If gravity were one affect, it would be a source of sorrow to our host planet, for the Earth is powerfully moved by the Sun and the Sun responds but little.

7 Though the Constitution speaks of freedom in a political context, in my private language, I distinguish between freedom as an inner capacity, seated in the soul and effected by the will, and liberty as an external endowment located in public space and protected by law.

8 Abraham Lincoln, "The Perpetuation of Our Political Institutions: Address before the Young Men's Lyceum of Springfield, Illinois" (1838).

9 Conversations, as distinct from discussions, in which point-making and -winning are involved. Conversations rely on receptive listening and mutual help. They depend on faith in a common humanity *as well as* a unique personality.

10 I was already grateful that he had not intended to derail the conversation from theoretical fundamentals to the current preoccupations, race and gender—which tend to be most energetic when, even because, the cause has all but triumphed—when it's no longer so costly.

11 Arthur Schlesinger, "The Lost Meaning of 'The Pursuit of Happiness,'" *A Casebook on the Declaration of Independence*, ed. Robert Ginsberg (1967), p. 217.

12　Thomas Hobbes, *Leviathan* (1651), Pt. I, Ch. XI. This quotation might well be the source for the "chase" theory of happiness. To me it is a prescription for misery.

13　Plato, *Republic*, 414 c – 415 a. Socrates proposes his notion of the human soul-metals as a "royal lie," but the lie is not in souls being made of differently valued soul-metal, but in the claim that the philosopher-kings can assess souls reliably. Socrates seems to me here to acknowledge the most positive preachment of virtuous egalitarianism: there is to be generally respectful conduct. Absent much time and many occasions we just don't know what people "are made of." Yet Socrates' "beauty-city" (*kallipolis* 527 c) is constructed as an aristocracy with its castes. But it is, *explicitly,* not intended as a constitution for a real city-founding, but as a plan for a soul's self-founding (592 b); it is a psychology writ large, which *is* meant to be lived out.

Is anyone a true believer in the actual equality of souls, since it is, to begin with, conceptually inconceivable? (See the argument in the text below.) Even Jefferson, who managed to speak of "lovely equality" (letter to John Bannister, 1787) can bring himself to refer to the gifted as being "raked from the rubbish" (*Notes on the State of Virginia*, 1782, Query XIV). And even the "We" of the Declaration has a soupçon of the royal we.

14　Quite new. Our dollar bills say: *Novus ordo seclorum*, "A new order of the ages"—a new time order, a restart of history.

15 Tocqueville observed a democratic "love" for equality as furnishing "a multitude of little enjoyments daily to each man." He is describing just the positive good into which I am inquiring, and he thinks that this love is "ardent, insatiable, eternal," whereas the attachment to freedom is merely "a natural taste" (Vol. II, Pt. ii, Ch. 1).

16 Aristotle, *Politics* 1255 a 10.

17 *Shared* here means not *shared out*, "divided up," but *share in*, "own together."

18 The theological term for "aboriginal debasement" might be "original sin." Many of us have an internal resonance, a psychic hum—not unlike that cosmic background noise, that remains of a past event beyond our individual experience. It signifies a constitutional human unease. So we say: "I did my best." We rarely did.

19 Friedrich Nietzsche, *Beyond Good and Evil* (1886), for example, in connection with equality and honors: Ch. VI, no. 212. Nietzsche is exonerated from his clever but ultimately clueless attacks on democracy by getting the epiphenomena hilariously right.

20 I do think that the one way to know what other people have in their minds is to be told by them—but only if it is confided in that secular confession, a trusting conversation, and the confessional stall is a moving car, and hearing is by turns.

One more: I am thinking of those fellow-humans for whom both personal and political equality is an ideal state, an absolute good, pursued even in the face of a common come-down, for its own sake. They are ready to suspend plans promising positive improvement for relative rectification and to subordinate freedom to sameness. A chief error in the cry of the French Revolution, of which equality is the centerpiece, *Liberté, Egalité, Fraternité,* seems to me to be the implication that the three notions aid and abet each other. But most happy siblings are unequal in age and it is this complementarity rather than equality of condition that often makes for the most poignant brotherliness—or sisterhood.

In any case, fraternity was only occasionally a member of this triple ejaculation. One consequence, probably not entirely unintended, of this, as of any such cry, is that no one can tell what relation the terms might have to each other. No two notions in politics could be more doubtfully connected— do they support or suppress each other?—than liberty and equality. At the risk of being obvious: Where equality is to be maintained, certain liberties have to be curtailed; where liberty is to be actual, inequality has to be allowed.

21 A less rabid but very authoritative plea for inequality is attributed by an Englishman to another Greek, albeit an imaginary one, Ulysses (Odysseus in Homer—best-loved by me, together with an ultra-real one, Socrates). Shakespeare coopts him for a long speech containing, centrally, these lines:

> O! When degree is shak'd,
> Which is the ladder of all high designs,
> The enterprise is sick. How could communities,
> Degrees in schools, and brotherhood in cities,
> Peaceful commerce from dividable shores,
> The primogeniture and due of birth,
> Prerogative of age, crowns, sceptres, laurels,
> But by degree, stand in authentic place?
> Take but degree away, untune that string,
> And, hark! What discord follows; each thing meets
> In mere oppugnancy…
>
> *Troilus and Cressida* I iii 109 ff.

Note that in the fourth line Ulysses exactly contradicts the connection of equality and fraternity of Note 20. Actually, Shakespeare has the exactly right intuition in making him the eloquent defender of rank ("degree"). In the *Iliad* his avatar Odysseus is, although himself a king, continually obliged to defend from incipient rebellion his overlord Agamemnon, who is incompetent and a royally pompous ass. And he does so loyally and because he fears *mere oppugnancy*, "nothing but infighting."

22 Covenanted: Recall that shortly after birth the male child was circumcised and therewith entered into a Covenant with God (*Genesis* 18:11–12). It was also the day of the boy's naming, and that raises the interesting question why America is not named in the speech; Lincoln may have refrained from

naming the "United States" out of tact—Confederate soldiers were also buried in the cemetery where he gave the speech.

23 To the point: Helmut Shoeck, *Envy: A Theory of Social Behavior* (1966), trans. from German by Martin Secker (1987). The subtitle is revealing. Envy is an anti-social way of socializing. The longest indexical entries are under Equality and Inequality, clearly the main attractors of this propensity. Aristotle on envy: *Rhetoric* II 9, 10.

Two essays bearing on equality, very helpful: Michael N. Fried (Ben Gurion University of the Negev), "Similarity and Equality in Euclid and Apollonius" (2013); Barry Mazur (Harvard University), "When is one thing equal to some other thing?" (2007: equivalence, i.e., isomorphism, supersedes equality).

24 Thus Max Scheler: "'Equality,' as a purely rational idea can never stimulate desire, will, or emotion" (*Envy*, p. 282). But it can; it does! Freud differs. He claims that sibling rivalry, here the older child's envy of the love the newcomer receives, is the cause of its sense of group solidarity. Having lost its primary position in the family, the child transfers its allegiance to the troop of children in the same predicament (ibid., p. 81). In other words, democrats are generated by sibling rivalry, the source of egalitarian allegiance!

25 Friedrich Nietzsche, *The Will to Power* (a postmortem collection, n. 864, and *passim*).

26   The invasion of our Capital by a mob on Wednesday, January 6, 2021, was followed by expressions of a public sentiment that served to instantiate "secular reverence."

27   My prime example, the normal reference to the state of mutual attachment as a *relationship*, is not a meaning listed in my Oxford English Dictionary of 1971. I infer that it is more recent. Why would we describe ourselves with this term, since we are *ipso facto* in a relationship with everybody we come across. It is, unintendedly, devaluing to refer to—I was about to write "something special," but that locution has exactly the same problem—a condition of great consequence in such least-common-denominator terms.

28   Benefits: the chief of which, quite aside from great material advantages, seems to me to be that to a really educated person (a condition that bears no relation to a diploma) practically everything is interesting. Interest bestows some immunity against boredom. Boredom is, to my mind, the most dangerous human passion—the passion that is an a-pathy. It breeds self-harm and violence, civil unrest and war.

29   There are, to be sure, two views of the power of ideas, polar opposites. Some think that ideas, essences, are indeed pulled away, "drawn off," *abstracted from real things*, from "thingly" things. Others, myself included, conjecture that these *realia* are—somehow—spawned, brought into being, by ideas, which are thus concrete in the extreme: stable in

duration, dense in quality, potent in generation—and not entirely inaccessible to the human intellect.

30 Proclus, *Commentary on the First Book of Euclid's* Elements (c. 450 C.E.), trans. Glenn Morrow, ¶52–53: [The imagination] "thinks the circle as extended, and although this circle is free of extended matter, it possesses an intelligible matter provided by the imagination itself." Aristotle had spoken in the *Metaphysics* of a *hyle aisthete* and *noete*, a "sensory" and an "intellectual matter" (1036 a).

31 I have misgivings about the locution "material things" as opposed to ensouled animals. Is a book or a piece of music properly described as a "material thing"? Isn't there a whiff of soul about them? Why would evil actors burn books if they were not intending murder? Another misgiving: Just below I'll be considering greed, although if it is, say, for self-knowledge, it is, if well-conducted, good. By "well-conducted" I mean something like a Socratic *psychology* invested in delineating the soul with "complete accuracy" and asking if it is a unity or multiplicity (*Phaedo* 271 a), not a Freudian *psychiatry* concerned with its discontents.

32 My limited experience stems from being twice on a school board whose fellow members were millionaires. A standard conversation: My colleague, with the somewhat disconcerted respect some rich people have for academics, "I've always wanted to be a teacher; it must be so rewarding!" Me, appreciatively, out

loud: "Yes, so it is," and silently, "Then what kept you?"

33 Herodotus, *Persian Wars*, quotes a Persian law: "The King may do whatever he wishes" (III 31). "King of kings" signifies that the Persian King is sovereign over the multitude of ethnic kings, all equally, just lower-case kings.

34 I learned far too late that we're not entitled to make a general pronouncement, no matter how justifiable, unless we can produce one of the cases, real or ideal, which induced it.

35 "The communion of incommensurables": the antithesis of a locution used by a recent failed presidential candidate: a "basket of deplorables." "Incommensurable" fits; that is, insofar human being is simply not measurable by rational, sayable numbers—nor any others.

36 E. B., *Un-Willing* (2014), Conclusion C2.

37 The classical texts are: Aristotle, *Nicomachean Ethics,* III 2 and Thomas Aquinas, *Summa Theologica*, Pt. 1, Qq. 80, 82. Further texts in *Un-Willing*, p. 271, n. 31.

Poetry as intellectual activity *and* love-driven: Some critics can't believe it; they think that serious thinking always occurs in the *critical* mode and conclude that the greatest sonnet-sequence in English had no definitively determinable addressee; it was not aimed at a lover but at producing an expert's *jeu d'esprit,* a poetic *tour de force*. Some diversion!

38 "Conceiving possibilities": Aristotle (*Nicomachean Ethics*) says we take ends for granted and don't deliberate about them. Well, perhaps not in that sense of deliberating which is making choices. But we do muse, meditate about ends so as to discover possibilities, formulate them, and let one come to the fore. In acting well, more than ever, well-begun is half done. For to know what you want "for good" is surely the ballast of life.

39 In my childhood in Berlin in the thirties, a book called *The Malice of the Object* (*Die Tücke des Objects*), whose author I don't recall, was popular. It explained in anthropomorphic terms why, if you drop an open-face sandwich, it falls on the liverwurst side; as Herodotus would say: "For my part, I believe it was because the breeze it made falling flipped it."

40 Behavior can be voluntary, a sort of passive will, assent to the given; Aristotle, *Nicomachean Ethics* III 1: *hekousion,* "willing." No Greek or Latin word precisely corresponding to modern will, a kind of mental exertion of force, carries that meaning until Augustine (in the late fourth century C.E.) first formulates it in *On Free Choice* (*De Libero Arbitrio*) as a self-directed power with a capacity for perversion, for rebellion against God (III 13). Thus willfulness was the first version of modern will. Augustine as a Christian, being a post-Pagan, was a proto-modern. Quite incidentally, the early Stoics were our very close forerunners in antiquity (E. B. *Feeling our Feelings: What Philosophers Think and People*

Know, 2008, Ch. IV 2). They invented cognitive representa-
tionalism, the dominant theory of knowledge in modernity.

Not so incidentally: Augustine gives literary form to the understanding of thinking Socrates sets out in the *Theaetetus*
as "the account that the soul goes through with itself concerning that which it is inspecting" (189 e). Augustine calls
it *soliloquia*, a conversation of one, *solus—not with himself
but with his reason.* Note that Socrates speaks of the soul,
our own inner being, conversing with itself. Christian Augustine's emendation—we are having a solus conversation
not with our soul but with our *reason*—seems to me *deeply*
significant, but I haven't grasped its meaning yet.

The relevance of this historical note to my thesis is that I'm
about to appeal to the will for an engagement with equality.

One last observation: In English the lexical relation of "will"
to the future of the verb "to be" shifts the coloration of the
ancient terms (Gk. *boule*, Lat. *voluntas*) somewhat from
"working one's will" to "planning for the future." Yet later
though the Victorians still spoke of breaking children's will,
we encourage them to practice some willpower.

41 I am referring to an anthology devoted to the linguistic
movement that blossomed in the early second half of the last
century: *The Linguistic Turn: Recent Essays in Philosophical
Method*, edited and introduced by Richard Rorty (1967). This
movement sought in linguistic reform the solution to all the

apparently insoluble metaphysical problems of professional philosophy. To me, it seems natural that there were no solutions to these "problems." They weren't problems, that's why. *Problems* are formulated to dissolve upon solution. If we have a problem, say with cockroaches, we want it, we want them, to go away. These metaphysical concerns are *questions*, and we want to dwell in, with them—because they aren't just "interesting," they are what it means to "be among" (*inter-esse*), all that surrounds us outside and sustains us within.

Moreover, I am innocent of a method since a procedure jigs the inquiry and so the outcome. Nor can I believe that speech can *reform* thinking, to me it seems that *Logos,* articulable reason, should *inform* speech.

42 It's so with dogs, for example (not to speak of cockroaches). Even breeds aren't always distinguishing marks. People are more apt to say: "He's a dog-owner" than "He's a Pekinese-owner," probably because they can't tell many breeds apart. Individual dogs do have their ways, mostly evident to their owners, but they don't undergo that persistent progress in individualization we do—especially when we stop trying. Actually, a real education helps; it has a dual effect: more individual distinction and more comprehensive humanity.

43 Alexander Hamilton, in *Federalist*, No. 78, says something relevant to my argument for the will's potent agency. In defending the Constitution's lifetime appointments for Fed-

eral judges, he argues that they "may truly be said to have no Force nor Will, but merely judgment; …" That dictum confirms—it was always clear—that as we humans are endowed with judgment *attached* to a will, we become the most potent, not "the least dangerous," of functionaries in our world.

44   Will, the capacity (it is not, as I've reported, a faculty but an ability achieved by the melding of desire and reason) has its own *strong* verb, "to will," with meanings from wanting to commanding, as in a sentence somewhere in Shakespeare. "I will none of thee," and a made-up sample sentence: "She willed the book into being."

Then there is the *auxiliary* verb mentioned in the text, as in "I will [am going to] do it." Here you can see why an alternative future, "going to," is needed since "I will" is ambiguous; it could be meant strongly: "It is my will to do it."

There is a usage, now in abeyance, but I shall revive it next time occasion offers: The future of "to be" was differently inflected from the future of "to will." For example, the future first person singular of "to be" was "I shall," but of "to will" it was "I will." Then in the second and third persons, it flips; thus "you shall do it" is a command and "you will do it" a prognosis. The workaround for all that is "I'll do it, you'll do it."

45   E. B., *The World of the Imagination: Sum and Substance* (1991, 25th Anniversary Edition, 2017), Pt. Six, Ch. II c. I argue that the imagination is inherently past-related and -nour-

ished, because there, in the past, is temporally located "whatever has passed into and through the memorial workshop of the soul," and is thus Past.

46 Heraclitus B 123, in Hermann Diels, Walther Kranz, *Fragmente der Vorsokratiker* (1954).

47 I hasten to say that large public meetings, be they celebratory or mournful or dissenting, can be civically exhilarating—if the dominant spirit is moderate.

G. W. F. Hegel's analysis of the thought movements of radical egalitarianism of the French Revolution and its terrible culmination are very convincingly set out in *The Phenomenology of the Spirit* (1807), "Absolute Freedom and Terror" (Spirit, B. III; in this book Hegel never gives the historical epoch-name). *Liberté, Egalité, Fraternité,* as mentioned above, was the cry of the age; the staccato ejaculation ensures that the deep political problem—whether liberty and equality are practically compatible—is suppressed. "Brotherhood" is a weak member of the trio; it often doesn't appear in citations.

48 A book setting out the modern mania for measurement and its human (or, better, de-humanizing) consequences is Steffen Mau, *The Metric Society: On the Quantification of the Social,* trans. from German by Sharon Howe, Polity Press (2019).

49 On selfhood: Richard Sorabji, *Self: Ancient and Modern Insights about Individuality, Life and Death* (2006).

To me, the "problem" of self seems more like the question of questions—indeed more like a mystery, almost on the same level of attracting and confounding the intellect as is the idea of a three-in-one, each itself and each all, presented by the Christian Trinity.

Because "agency," the intellect's activity reaching into the world, seems to me to be one element of personhood—the other being receptivity, a sort of responsive passivity. I have no faith in thinkers, like Nietzsche, who replace divinity with an impersonal Will (working, to be sure, from below rather than from above). A will needs a person to dwell in.

50 Richard Dedekind, in his classical essay "Continuity and Irrational Numbers" (1872) repairs, so to speak, the absence of a common measure ("incommensurability"), since neither natural nor rational (fractional) numbers will do, by introducing "irrational" numbers, a new type.

51 The "Terrible Twos" are the first appearance of our sense that we are our own first and last resort. Soon after pre-verbal infancy there is an explosion of mere willing, willfulness, willing for its own sake. The fact that it is a normal developmental stage betokens that, as embodied souls, nature has set us on a path to a mature, a free will, which is not to ride us but to be exercised by us.

52 *Die Gedanken sind frei, wer kann sie erraten?*
Sie fliegen vorbei wie nächtliche Schatten.
Kein Mensch kann sie wissen, Kein Jäger erschiessen

Es bleibet dabei: Die Gedanken sind frei.

53 There is a set of publicly potent notions that is *essentially* contentless by reason of being procedure- or method-related. They deserve a book, one item in which would be the unintended consequences, good or bad, of turning such conceptions into programs. For example, it has been plausibly argued that the more a government is confined to mere administration, to implementing law and the less to enforcing content—for example, notions of virtue, righteousness, and morality, the safer our liberty is. In any case, preachments are only half-efficacious. To some degree they invoke recalcitrance and silent seething in the majority (usually, these days) whose way of life is, by implication, being impugned. Once more: Silent seething is dangerous.

On worldly time as a mere formalism that attracts a way of talking as if it had being and power when it is a mere consequence of motion's measurability, see E. B., *What, Then, Is Time?* (1999), Ch. 1.

54 Identity: In this essay I have concentrated on those natural rights, that is, those bestowed by Nature or "Nature's God" (Preamble, Declaration), that are closely related to equality, imperfect identity, because people may be very diverse but

identical in some proportion, first among them their common species, that is, *homo sapiens*, the only extant species of our primate family, the Hominidae. This species, our humanity, belongs unexceptionably and equally to all of us, except in figurative language, such as "man's 'inhumanity' (that is, beastliness) to man." We can no more renounce our species than we can, pace Lady Macbeth (I v 48), "unsex" ourselves.

The recent identity movements, however, insist on a different sort of right, not from nature and birth, but by law and medical intervention. Candidacy is by personal decision and a claim of tribal belonging. It speaks to the attractive power of equality that even here it sometimes prevails and movements ostensibly devoted to tribal rights end up more devoted to social equality (*The Economist*, 1/16/21, in France).

Identity is not always compatible with equality, since in the political realm the out-group is apt to regard itself as being what might be called pain-privileged, distinguished by superior suffering. The suppressed predicate here is the implicit trust the oppressed minorities (which are small percentage-wise) place in the common kindliness of the non-tribal majority, for example, its willingness to respond positively to protests.

A postlude: Identity politics is not alien to the Constitution. All states, be they large or small in population, have, equally, two senators. Dwellers in the small states, a minority, thus form a smallness-tribe, identified by being few per square mile; it is, in fact, an identifiable human mode as well; the Montanans I know are the strong silent type and regard steak as a breakfast food.

55 Discussed in E. B. *Feigning*, Ch. IV, J. (Paul Dry Books, 2021).

56 I am thinking of the Paleolithic cave paintings in the Dordogne, which offer the experience of a lifetime. For these painters were consummate representationalists; their aurochs are living oxen and high art at once.

57 The "dinosaurs" who value voting in person over going online, are driven, it seems, by some such sentiment. As a child in Berlin, in the early thirties, before the Nazi catastrophe fully hit the Jews, I used to walk, hand in hand with my father, to the polling place; he was a *Sozialdemokrat.*

58 It is curious that, although "diversity" is the mantra of our time, yet social and economic disparity, great spawners of human diversity, are disparaged.

59 I am speaking of a modern type. In antiquity there was conceivable a pure intellect so humanly integrated that it devolved its judgments directly to its own executing body, no will required. (See E. B., *Un-Willing*, Ch. 1, "Before Will.")

60 A friend of mine—English—who served very moderately apportioned meals, referred to them as being of "an elegant

sufficiency." It's not the sufficiency I mean. "Enough" has to have enough plenitude to make some sort of satisfaction, some version of happiness, possible. In time of crisis it may mean throwing the country deep into hock to supply enough for those in need.